50 Homemade High-Protein Breakfast Recipes for Home

By: Kelly Johnson

Table of Contents

- Protein-Packed Breakfast Burrito
- Greek Yogurt Parfait with Nuts and Berries
- Veggie and Egg Scramble
- Peanut Butter Banana Protein Smoothie
- Quinoa Breakfast Bowl with Eggs and Avocado
- Protein Pancakes with Greek Yogurt and Berries
- Egg White Omelette with Spinach and Feta
- Cottage Cheese Pancakes with Fruit Compote
- Tofu Scramble with Vegetables
- Breakfast Egg Muffins with Turkey Sausage and Cheese
- Protein-Packed Oatmeal with Almond Butter and Chia Seeds
- High-Protein Breakfast Cookies with Protein Powder
- Chickpea Flour Pancakes with Blueberries
- Protein Waffles with Cottage Cheese
- Smoked Salmon and Avocado Toast
- Spinach and Mushroom Frittata
- Protein-Packed Chia Seed Pudding with Greek Yogurt
- Breakfast Quinoa Bowl with Almonds and Honey
- Turkey and Egg Breakfast Sandwich
- Protein-Packed Banana Bread with Whey Protein Powder
- High-Protein Breakfast Wrap with Chicken and Vegetables
- Chocolate Protein Overnight Oats with Almond Milk
- Egg White Breakfast Burrito with Black Beans and Salsa
- Protein-Packed Breakfast Casserole with Turkey Bacon and Cheese
- Peanut Butter Protein Balls with Rolled Oats and Honey
- Protein-Packed Green Smoothie with Kale and Hemp Seeds
- Baked Eggs in Avocado with Bacon
- Protein-Packed Breakfast Bagel with Cream Cheese and Smoked Salmon
- Quinoa Protein Pancakes with Cottage Cheese
- Breakfast Power Bowl with Sweet Potato and Black Beans
- High-Protein Banana Nut Muffins with Greek Yogurt
- Protein-Packed Breakfast Tacos with Egg and Beans
- Blueberry Protein Muffins with Whey Protein Powder
- Veggie and Tofu Breakfast Stir-Fry
- Protein-Packed French Toast with Whole Wheat Bread

- Protein Oat Bars with Almond Butter and Protein Powder
- Breakfast Egg Cups with Ham and Cheese
- Protein-Packed Breakfast Pizza with Egg and Turkey Bacon
- Protein-Packed Breakfast Sushi with Smoked Salmon and Avocado
- High-Protein Breakfast Trifle with Greek Yogurt and Granola
- Cottage Cheese and Fruit Bowl with Almonds
- Protein-Packed Breakfast Crepes with Cottage Cheese Filling
- Baked Protein Oatmeal with Apples and Cinnamon
- Egg and Turkey Sausage Breakfast Burrito Bowl
- High-Protein Breakfast Shake with Banana and Peanut Butter
- Protein-Packed Breakfast Bars with Quinoa and Nuts
- Breakfast Quesadilla with Egg, Cheese, and Black Beans
- Protein-Packed Breakfast Bread with Sunflower Seeds and Pumpkin Seeds
- Peanut Butter Protein Pancakes with Greek Yogurt Topping
- High-Protein Breakfast Smoothie Bowl with Spinach and Berries

Protein-Packed Breakfast Burrito

Ingredients:

- 2 large whole wheat or spinach tortillas
- 4 large eggs
- 1/2 cup black beans, drained and rinsed
- 1/4 cup diced bell peppers (any color)
- 1/4 cup diced onion
- 1/2 cup shredded cheddar cheese or Mexican blend cheese
- 1/4 cup salsa
- 1/4 cup chopped fresh cilantro (optional)
- Salt and pepper to taste
- Cooking oil or cooking spray

Instructions:

1. Heat a skillet over medium heat and add a little cooking oil or cooking spray.
2. In a bowl, whisk the eggs until well beaten. Season with salt and pepper to taste.
3. Pour the beaten eggs into the skillet and scramble them until they are fully cooked. Remove from the skillet and set aside.
4. In the same skillet, add a little more oil if needed and sauté the diced bell peppers and onions until they are softened.
5. Add the black beans to the skillet and cook for an additional 2-3 minutes, or until heated through.
6. Warm the tortillas in the microwave or on a skillet for a few seconds to make them pliable.
7. Divide the scrambled eggs, sautéed vegetables, and black beans evenly between the two tortillas.
8. Sprinkle shredded cheese on top of each burrito.
9. Add salsa and chopped cilantro on top, if desired.
10. Fold the sides of each tortilla over the filling, then roll up tightly to form a burrito.
11. Place the burritos seam-side down on the skillet and cook for 2-3 minutes on each side, or until golden brown and crispy.
12. Remove from the skillet and serve immediately.

These protein-packed breakfast burritos are versatile and can be customized with your favorite ingredients such as avocado, spinach, or diced tomatoes. They are perfect for a quick and nutritious breakfast on the go!

Greek Yogurt Parfait with Nuts and Berries

Ingredients:

- 1 cup Greek yogurt (plain or flavored)
- 1/2 cup mixed berries (such as strawberries, blueberries, raspberries)
- 2 tablespoons chopped nuts (such as almonds, walnuts, or pecans)
- 1 tablespoon honey or maple syrup (optional, for sweetness)
- Granola (optional, for added crunch)

Instructions:

1. Start by preparing your ingredients. Wash the berries and pat them dry with a paper towel. If using larger berries like strawberries, you can slice them into smaller pieces if desired. Chop the nuts if they're not already chopped.
2. In a bowl or glass, layer the Greek yogurt, mixed berries, and chopped nuts.
3. If desired, drizzle honey or maple syrup over the parfait for added sweetness.
4. Repeat the layers until you've used up all the ingredients, ending with a layer of berries and nuts on top.
5. Optionally, sprinkle granola over the top for added crunch and texture.
6. Serve the Greek yogurt parfait immediately as a nutritious and satisfying breakfast or snack.

This Greek yogurt parfait is packed with protein from the Greek yogurt and healthy fats from the nuts, making it a filling and balanced meal. The berries add natural sweetness and a burst of antioxidants, while the granola provides crunch and fiber. Feel free to customize the parfait with your favorite fruits, nuts, and toppings to suit your taste preferences!

Veggie and Egg Scramble

Ingredients:

- 4 large eggs
- 1 tablespoon olive oil or butter
- 1/2 cup diced bell peppers (any color)
- 1/2 cup diced onion
- 1/2 cup diced tomatoes
- 1 cup fresh spinach leaves
- Salt and pepper to taste
- Optional toppings: shredded cheese, sliced avocado, chopped fresh herbs

Instructions:

1. In a bowl, crack the eggs and whisk them together until well beaten. Season with salt and pepper to taste.
2. Heat the olive oil or butter in a skillet over medium heat.
3. Add the diced bell peppers and onions to the skillet and cook for 2-3 minutes, or until softened.
4. Add the diced tomatoes to the skillet and cook for an additional 1-2 minutes, or until slightly softened.
5. Add the fresh spinach leaves to the skillet and cook, stirring occasionally, until wilted.
6. Pour the beaten eggs into the skillet with the vegetables. Let the eggs cook undisturbed for a minute or so, then use a spatula to gently scramble them, stirring occasionally, until they are cooked to your desired consistency.
7. Once the eggs are cooked through, remove the skillet from the heat.
8. Taste the veggie and egg scramble and adjust the seasoning if needed.
9. Serve the veggie and egg scramble hot, topped with optional toppings such as shredded cheese, sliced avocado, or chopped fresh herbs.

This veggie and egg scramble is a quick and nutritious breakfast or brunch option that's packed with protein and loaded with colorful vegetables. Feel free to customize the recipe by adding your favorite veggies or spices to suit your taste preferences!

Peanut Butter Banana Protein Smoothie

Ingredients:

- 1 ripe banana, peeled and sliced
- 1 tablespoon peanut butter (creamy or crunchy)
- 1 scoop vanilla protein powder
- 1 cup unsweetened almond milk or milk of your choice
- 1/2 cup Greek yogurt (plain or vanilla flavored)
- 1 tablespoon honey or maple syrup (optional, for extra sweetness)
- Handful of ice cubes

Instructions:

1. Place all the ingredients in a blender.
2. Blend on high speed until smooth and creamy, scraping down the sides of the blender as needed to ensure all ingredients are well incorporated.
3. Taste the smoothie and adjust sweetness if needed by adding more honey or maple syrup.
4. If you prefer a thicker smoothie, you can add more ice cubes or a frozen banana.
5. Pour the peanut butter banana protein smoothie into glasses and serve immediately.
6. Optionally, you can garnish the smoothie with a sprinkle of cinnamon or a drizzle of additional peanut butter for extra flavor.

This peanut butter banana protein smoothie is not only delicious but also packed with protein, healthy fats, and carbohydrates, making it a satisfying and nutritious breakfast or snack option. Enjoy it post-workout or as a quick pick-me-up during the day!

Quinoa Breakfast Bowl with Eggs and Avocado

Ingredients:

- 1/2 cup quinoa, rinsed
- 1 cup water or vegetable broth
- 2 large eggs
- 1 ripe avocado, sliced
- 1/2 cup cherry tomatoes, halved
- 1/4 cup diced red onion
- 1/4 cup chopped fresh cilantro or parsley
- Juice of 1/2 lime
- Salt and pepper to taste
- Optional toppings: salsa, hot sauce, crumbled feta or goat cheese, sliced jalapeños

Instructions:

1. In a small saucepan, combine the quinoa and water or vegetable broth. Bring to a boil, then reduce the heat to low, cover, and simmer for 15-20 minutes, or until the quinoa is cooked and the liquid is absorbed. Fluff the quinoa with a fork and set aside.
2. While the quinoa is cooking, bring a medium pot of water to a gentle simmer. Carefully crack the eggs into the simmering water and poach them for 3-4 minutes, or until the whites are set but the yolks are still runny. Use a slotted spoon to remove the poached eggs from the water and drain them on a paper towel.
3. In a medium mixing bowl, combine the cooked quinoa, sliced avocado, halved cherry tomatoes, diced red onion, and chopped fresh cilantro or parsley. Squeeze the lime juice over the mixture and season with salt and pepper to taste. Toss gently to combine.
4. Divide the quinoa mixture between two bowls. Top each bowl with a poached egg and any optional toppings you like, such as salsa, hot sauce, crumbled feta or goat cheese, or sliced jalapeños.
5. Serve the quinoa breakfast bowls immediately, with additional lime wedges on the side if desired.

This quinoa breakfast bowl with eggs and avocado is packed with protein, fiber, and healthy fats, making it a nutritious and satisfying way to start your day. Feel free to customize the recipe with your favorite vegetables, herbs, and toppings to suit your taste preferences!

Protein Pancakes with Greek Yogurt and Berries

Ingredients:

For the pancakes:

- 1 cup rolled oats
- 1 ripe banana
- 2 large eggs
- 1/2 cup Greek yogurt
- 1 scoop vanilla protein powder
- 1 teaspoon baking powder
- 1/2 teaspoon ground cinnamon
- Pinch of salt
- 1 tablespoon honey or maple syrup (optional, for sweetness)
- Cooking oil or butter, for greasing the skillet

For serving:

- Greek yogurt
- Mixed berries (such as strawberries, blueberries, raspberries)
- Honey or maple syrup (optional, for drizzling)
- Chopped nuts or seeds (such as almonds, walnuts, or chia seeds) (optional, for topping)

Instructions:

1. In a blender or food processor, combine the rolled oats, ripe banana, eggs, Greek yogurt, vanilla protein powder, baking powder, cinnamon, salt, and honey or maple syrup (if using). Blend until smooth and well combined, scraping down the sides of the blender as needed.
2. Heat a non-stick skillet or griddle over medium heat. Lightly grease the skillet with cooking oil or butter.
3. Pour the pancake batter onto the skillet to form pancakes of your desired size. Cook for 2-3 minutes, or until bubbles start to form on the surface of the pancakes and the edges look set.

4. Flip the pancakes and cook for an additional 1-2 minutes on the other side, or until golden brown and cooked through.
5. Remove the pancakes from the skillet and repeat with the remaining batter, greasing the skillet as needed.
6. To serve, stack the protein pancakes on plates. Top each stack with a dollop of Greek yogurt and a handful of mixed berries. Drizzle with honey or maple syrup if desired, and sprinkle with chopped nuts or seeds for added crunch and texture.
7. Serve the protein pancakes with Greek yogurt and berries immediately, while warm.

These protein pancakes with Greek yogurt and berries are a delicious and nutritious breakfast option that's packed with protein, fiber, and vitamins. They're perfect for fueling your day and keeping you satisfied until your next meal! Feel free to customize the toppings with your favorite fruits, nuts, and seeds.

Egg White Omelette with Spinach and Feta

Ingredients:

- 4 large egg whites
- 1 cup fresh spinach leaves, chopped
- 1/4 cup crumbled feta cheese
- 1 tablespoon olive oil or butter
- Salt and pepper to taste
- Optional: chopped fresh herbs (such as parsley or dill) for garnish

Instructions:

1. In a bowl, whisk the egg whites until frothy. Season with salt and pepper to taste.
2. Heat the olive oil or butter in a non-stick skillet over medium heat.
3. Add the chopped spinach to the skillet and cook for 1-2 minutes, or until wilted.
4. Pour the whisked egg whites into the skillet, tilting the pan to spread them evenly over the spinach.
5. Cook the egg whites for 2-3 minutes, or until they start to set around the edges.
6. Using a spatula, gently lift the edges of the omelette and tilt the skillet to allow any uncooked egg to flow underneath.
7. Once the egg whites are mostly set but still slightly runny on top, sprinkle the crumbled feta cheese evenly over one half of the omelette.
8. Carefully fold the other half of the omelette over the cheese, creating a half-moon shape.
9. Cook the omelette for an additional 1-2 minutes, or until the cheese is melted and the egg whites are fully cooked through.
10. Slide the egg white omelette onto a plate and garnish with chopped fresh herbs if desired.
11. Serve the egg white omelette with spinach and feta hot, as a delicious and protein-packed breakfast or brunch option.

This egg white omelette with spinach and feta cheese is light, fluffy, and full of flavor.

It's a healthy and satisfying meal that's perfect for starting your day on the right foot!

Feel free to customize the omelette with additional vegetables or herbs to suit your taste preferences.

Cottage Cheese Pancakes with Fruit Compote

Ingredients:

For the pancakes:

- 1 cup cottage cheese
- 4 large eggs
- 1/4 cup all-purpose flour or oat flour
- 1 tablespoon honey or maple syrup
- 1 teaspoon vanilla extract
- 1/2 teaspoon baking powder
- Pinch of salt
- Butter or cooking oil, for greasing the skillet

For the fruit compote:

- 1 cup mixed berries (such as strawberries, blueberries, raspberries)
- 2 tablespoons honey or maple syrup
- 1 tablespoon lemon juice
- 1/2 teaspoon vanilla extract

Instructions:

For the pancakes:

1. In a blender or food processor, combine the cottage cheese, eggs, flour, honey or maple syrup, vanilla extract, baking powder, and salt. Blend until smooth and well combined.
2. Heat a non-stick skillet or griddle over medium heat. Grease the skillet with butter or cooking oil.
3. Pour the pancake batter onto the skillet to form pancakes of your desired size.
4. Cook the pancakes for 2-3 minutes on one side, or until bubbles start to form on the surface and the edges look set.

5. Flip the pancakes and cook for an additional 1-2 minutes on the other side, or until golden brown and cooked through.
6. Remove the pancakes from the skillet and keep them warm while you prepare the fruit compote.

For the fruit compote:

1. In a small saucepan, combine the mixed berries, honey or maple syrup, lemon juice, and vanilla extract.
2. Cook the mixture over medium heat, stirring occasionally, for 5-7 minutes, or until the berries start to break down and release their juices.
3. Use a fork or potato masher to lightly mash some of the berries, leaving some chunks for texture.
4. Remove the fruit compote from the heat and let it cool slightly.

To serve:

1. Stack the cottage cheese pancakes on plates.
2. Spoon the warm fruit compote over the pancakes.
3. Serve the cottage cheese pancakes with fruit compote immediately, as a delicious and nutritious breakfast or brunch option.

These cottage cheese pancakes with fruit compote are light, fluffy, and packed with protein, making them a satisfying and wholesome meal. Enjoy them with your favorite fruits and toppings for a delicious start to your day!

Tofu Scramble with Vegetables

Ingredients:

- 1 block (14-16 ounces) firm tofu, drained
- 2 tablespoons olive oil or cooking oil of choice
- 1/2 onion, diced
- 2 cloves garlic, minced
- 1 bell pepper, diced
- 1 cup mushrooms, sliced
- 1 cup spinach or kale, chopped
- 2 tablespoons nutritional yeast (optional, for a cheesy flavor)
- 1 teaspoon ground turmeric (for color)
- Salt and pepper to taste
- Optional toppings: chopped fresh herbs, avocado slices, hot sauce

Instructions:

1. Start by pressing the tofu to remove excess moisture. Wrap the tofu block in a clean kitchen towel or paper towels and place a heavy object on top (such as a cast iron skillet or a couple of canned goods). Let it sit for 15-20 minutes, then unwrap and crumble the tofu with your hands.
2. In a large skillet, heat the olive oil over medium heat. Add the diced onion and cook for 2-3 minutes, or until softened.
3. Add the minced garlic to the skillet and cook for an additional 1-2 minutes, or until fragrant.
4. Add the diced bell pepper and sliced mushrooms to the skillet. Cook for 5-7 minutes, or until the vegetables are softened and lightly browned.
5. Stir in the crumbled tofu, nutritional yeast (if using), and ground turmeric. Season with salt and pepper to taste.
6. Cook the tofu scramble for 5-7 minutes, stirring occasionally, until the tofu is heated through and any excess moisture has evaporated.
7. Add the chopped spinach or kale to the skillet and cook for an additional 2-3 minutes, or until wilted.
8. Taste the tofu scramble and adjust the seasoning if needed.
9. Remove the skillet from the heat and serve the tofu scramble hot, garnished with optional toppings such as chopped fresh herbs, avocado slices, or hot sauce.

This tofu scramble with vegetables is a nutritious and flavorful dish that's perfect for breakfast, brunch, or any meal of the day. It's packed with protein, fiber, and vitamins, making it a satisfying and wholesome option for vegans and vegetarians. Enjoy it on its own or with your favorite side dishes!

Breakfast Egg Muffins with Turkey Sausage and Cheese

Ingredients:

- 8 large eggs
- 1/4 cup milk (or non-dairy milk)
- 1/2 teaspoon salt
- 1/4 teaspoon black pepper
- 1/2 cup cooked turkey sausage, crumbled
- 1/2 cup shredded cheddar cheese (or cheese of your choice)
- 1/4 cup chopped green onions or chives
- Cooking spray or olive oil, for greasing the muffin tin

Instructions:

1. Preheat your oven to 375°F (190°C). Grease a 12-cup muffin tin with cooking spray or olive oil.
2. In a large mixing bowl, whisk together the eggs, milk, salt, and black pepper until well combined.
3. Stir in the cooked turkey sausage, shredded cheese, and chopped green onions or chives until evenly distributed throughout the egg mixture.
4. Pour the egg mixture evenly into the prepared muffin tin, filling each cup about 3/4 full.
5. Bake the breakfast egg muffins in the preheated oven for 20-25 minutes, or until the eggs are set and the tops are golden brown.
6. Remove the muffin tin from the oven and let the egg muffins cool for a few minutes before removing them from the tin.
7. Use a butter knife or spatula to gently loosen the edges of the egg muffins, then carefully lift them out of the muffin tin and transfer them to a wire rack to cool slightly.
8. Serve the breakfast egg muffins warm as a delicious and protein-packed breakfast option.

These breakfast egg muffins with turkey sausage and cheese are portable, convenient, and perfect for meal prep. They can be stored in an airtight container in the refrigerator for up to 3-4 days. Enjoy them on busy weekday mornings or as a grab-and-go snack any time of day!

Protein-Packed Oatmeal with Almond Butter and Chia Seeds

Ingredients:

- 1/2 cup rolled oats
- 1 cup water or milk (dairy or non-dairy)
- 1 tablespoon almond butter
- 1 tablespoon chia seeds
- 1/2 teaspoon ground cinnamon
- 1 tablespoon honey or maple syrup (optional, for sweetness)
- Fresh fruit, nuts, or seeds for topping (optional)

Instructions:

1. In a small saucepan, combine the rolled oats and water or milk. Bring to a boil over medium heat, then reduce the heat to low and simmer for 5-7 minutes, stirring occasionally, until the oats are cooked and the mixture has thickened to your desired consistency.
2. Stir in the almond butter, chia seeds, ground cinnamon, and honey or maple syrup (if using). Mix until well combined and heated through.
3. Remove the oatmeal from the heat and let it sit for a minute to thicken further.
4. Transfer the protein-packed oatmeal to a bowl and top with your favorite fresh fruit, nuts, or seeds for added flavor, texture, and nutrition.
5. Serve the oatmeal warm and enjoy immediately as a nutritious and satisfying breakfast option.

This protein-packed oatmeal with almond butter and chia seeds is rich in fiber, healthy fats, and protein, making it a filling and nourishing way to start your day. Customize the recipe with your favorite toppings and enjoy the delicious combination of flavors and textures!

High-Protein Breakfast Cookies with Protein Powder

Ingredients:

- 1 cup rolled oats
- 1/2 cup vanilla protein powder
- 1/4 cup almond flour or oat flour
- 1/4 cup chopped nuts (such as almonds, walnuts, or pecans)
- 1/4 cup dried fruit (such as raisins, cranberries, or chopped dates)
- 1/4 cup unsweetened shredded coconut
- 1/4 cup honey or maple syrup
- 1/4 cup almond butter or peanut butter
- 1/4 cup coconut oil, melted
- 1 large egg
- 1 teaspoon vanilla extract
- 1/2 teaspoon ground cinnamon
- 1/4 teaspoon salt

Instructions:

1. Preheat your oven to 350°F (175°C). Line a baking sheet with parchment paper or silicone baking mats.
2. In a large mixing bowl, combine the rolled oats, protein powder, almond flour or oat flour, chopped nuts, dried fruit, and shredded coconut.
3. In a separate microwave-safe bowl, combine the honey or maple syrup, almond butter or peanut butter, and coconut oil. Microwave for 30-60 seconds, or until the mixture is melted and smooth. Stir well to combine.
4. Add the melted nut butter mixture to the dry ingredients in the large mixing bowl. Stir until all the dry ingredients are evenly coated.
5. In a small bowl, whisk the egg with the vanilla extract, ground cinnamon, and salt.
6. Add the egg mixture to the large mixing bowl and stir until everything is well combined and forms a dough-like consistency.
7. Use a cookie scoop or spoon to portion the dough onto the prepared baking sheet, spacing the cookies evenly apart. Use your hands or the back of a spoon to flatten and shape each cookie.
8. Bake the high-protein breakfast cookies in the preheated oven for 12-15 minutes, or until the edges are golden brown and the cookies are set.

9. Remove the cookies from the oven and let them cool on the baking sheet for a few minutes before transferring them to a wire rack to cool completely.
10. Once cooled, store the high-protein breakfast cookies in an airtight container at room temperature for up to one week, or freeze them for longer storage.

These high-protein breakfast cookies with protein powder are perfect for a quick and nutritious breakfast on the go or a satisfying snack any time of day. They're loaded with protein, fiber, and healthy fats to keep you energized and satisfied. Enjoy them with a glass of milk or a cup of coffee for a delicious and convenient meal!

Chickpea Flour Pancakes with Blueberries

Ingredients:

- 1 cup chickpea flour
- 1 tablespoon coconut sugar or granulated sugar (optional)
- 1 teaspoon baking powder
- 1/2 teaspoon ground cinnamon (optional)
- Pinch of salt
- 1 cup almond milk or any milk of your choice
- 1 tablespoon melted coconut oil or cooking oil of your choice
- 1 teaspoon vanilla extract
- 1/2 cup fresh blueberries (or frozen, thawed)

Instructions:

1. In a large mixing bowl, whisk together the chickpea flour, coconut sugar (if using), baking powder, ground cinnamon (if using), and salt until well combined.
2. In a separate bowl, whisk together the almond milk, melted coconut oil, and vanilla extract.
3. Pour the wet ingredients into the dry ingredients and stir until just combined. Be careful not to overmix; a few lumps in the batter are okay.
4. Gently fold in the fresh blueberries until evenly distributed throughout the batter.
5. Let the batter rest for about 5-10 minutes to allow the chickpea flour to absorb the liquid and thicken slightly.
6. Heat a non-stick skillet or griddle over medium heat. Lightly grease the skillet with coconut oil or cooking spray.
7. Pour about 1/4 cup of the pancake batter onto the skillet for each pancake, spreading it out slightly with the back of a spoon if needed to form a circle.
8. Cook the pancakes for 2-3 minutes, or until bubbles start to form on the surface and the edges look set.
9. Carefully flip the pancakes and cook for an additional 1-2 minutes on the other side, or until golden brown and cooked through.
10. Repeat with the remaining batter, greasing the skillet as needed between batches.
11. Serve the chickpea flour pancakes with fresh blueberries on top and your favorite toppings, such as maple syrup, yogurt, or nut butter.

These chickpea flour pancakes with blueberries are naturally gluten-free, high in protein, and packed with fiber and nutrients. They make a delicious and nutritious breakfast or brunch option that everyone will love! Feel free to customize the recipe with your favorite fruits, nuts, or spices to suit your taste preferences. Enjoy!

Protein Waffles with Cottage Cheese

Ingredients:

- 1 cup cottage cheese
- 4 large eggs
- 1/4 cup milk (dairy or non-dairy)
- 1 teaspoon vanilla extract
- 1 tablespoon honey or maple syrup (optional)
- 1 cup oat flour (you can make your own by blending rolled oats until finely ground)
- 1 teaspoon baking powder
- Pinch of salt
- Cooking spray or oil for greasing the waffle iron

Instructions:

1. In a blender or food processor, combine the cottage cheese, eggs, milk, vanilla extract, and honey or maple syrup (if using). Blend until smooth.
2. In a large mixing bowl, whisk together the oat flour, baking powder, and salt.
3. Pour the wet ingredients from the blender into the bowl with the dry ingredients. Stir until just combined. Be careful not to overmix; a few lumps in the batter are okay.
4. Preheat your waffle iron according to the manufacturer's instructions. Once heated, lightly grease the waffle iron with cooking spray or oil.
5. Pour enough batter onto the preheated waffle iron to cover the surface, spreading it out slightly with a spoon or spatula if needed.
6. Close the waffle iron and cook the waffles according to the manufacturer's instructions, or until golden brown and crisp.
7. Carefully remove the waffles from the waffle iron and repeat with the remaining batter.
8. Serve the protein waffles warm with your favorite toppings, such as fresh fruit, yogurt, nut butter, or maple syrup.

These protein waffles with cottage cheese are a nutritious and delicious breakfast option that's packed with protein and fiber. They're easy to make and can be customized with your favorite toppings to suit your taste preferences. Enjoy them as a satisfying start to your day!

Smoked Salmon and Avocado Toast

Ingredients:

- 2 slices of your favorite bread (such as whole grain, sourdough, or rye)
- 1 ripe avocado
- 4 ounces smoked salmon
- Lemon juice
- Salt and pepper, to taste
- Optional toppings: fresh herbs (such as dill or chives), red onion slices, capers, microgreens

Instructions:

1. Toast the slices of bread until golden brown and crispy.
2. While the bread is toasting, prepare the avocado. Cut the avocado in half and remove the pit. Scoop the flesh into a bowl and mash it with a fork until smooth and creamy. Season with a squeeze of lemon juice, salt, and pepper to taste.
3. Once the bread is toasted, spread a generous layer of mashed avocado onto each slice.
4. Arrange the smoked salmon slices on top of the avocado.
5. Drizzle a little more lemon juice over the smoked salmon, if desired, and season with black pepper.
6. Garnish the toast with optional toppings such as fresh herbs, red onion slices, capers, or microgreens.
7. Serve the smoked salmon and avocado toast immediately, while the bread is still warm.

This smoked salmon and avocado toast makes for a delicious and satisfying breakfast, brunch, or light lunch option. It's packed with healthy fats, protein, and fiber, and the combination of creamy avocado and savory smoked salmon is simply irresistible. Enjoy!

Spinach and Mushroom Frittata

Ingredients:

- 8 large eggs
- 1/4 cup milk (dairy or non-dairy)
- Salt and pepper, to taste
- 1 tablespoon olive oil
- 1 small onion, diced
- 2 cloves garlic, minced
- 8 ounces mushrooms, sliced
- 2 cups fresh spinach leaves
- 1/2 cup shredded cheese (such as cheddar, mozzarella, or Gruyere)
- Optional toppings: chopped fresh herbs (such as parsley or chives), grated Parmesan cheese

Instructions:

1. Preheat your oven to 350°F (175°C).
2. In a large mixing bowl, whisk together the eggs, milk, salt, and pepper until well combined. Set aside.
3. Heat the olive oil in a 10-inch oven-safe skillet over medium heat.
4. Add the diced onion to the skillet and cook for 2-3 minutes, or until softened.
5. Add the minced garlic to the skillet and cook for an additional 1-2 minutes, or until fragrant.
6. Add the sliced mushrooms to the skillet and cook for 5-7 minutes, or until they release their moisture and start to brown.
7. Add the fresh spinach leaves to the skillet and cook, stirring occasionally, until wilted.
8. Pour the egg mixture into the skillet, covering the vegetables evenly.
9. Cook the frittata on the stovetop for 3-4 minutes, or until the edges start to set.
10. Sprinkle the shredded cheese evenly over the top of the frittata.
11. Transfer the skillet to the preheated oven and bake the frittata for 12-15 minutes, or until set in the center and lightly golden on top.
12. Remove the skillet from the oven and let the frittata cool for a few minutes before slicing.

13. Garnish the frittata with optional toppings such as chopped fresh herbs or grated Parmesan cheese.
14. Slice the frittata into wedges and serve warm or at room temperature.

This spinach and mushroom frittata is a versatile and satisfying dish that's perfect for breakfast, brunch, lunch, or dinner. It's packed with protein, vitamins, and minerals, and can be customized with your favorite vegetables and cheese. Enjoy!

Protein-Packed Chia Seed Pudding with Greek Yogurt

Ingredients:

- 1/4 cup chia seeds
- 1 cup unsweetened almond milk (or any milk of your choice)
- 1 cup Greek yogurt
- 1-2 tablespoons honey or maple syrup (optional, for sweetness)
- 1 teaspoon vanilla extract
- Optional toppings: fresh berries, sliced fruit, nuts, seeds, shredded coconut, honey or maple syrup

Instructions:

1. In a mixing bowl or jar, combine the chia seeds, almond milk, Greek yogurt, honey or maple syrup (if using), and vanilla extract. Stir well to combine.
2. Cover the bowl or jar and refrigerate the mixture for at least 2 hours, or preferably overnight, to allow the chia seeds to absorb the liquid and thicken into pudding.
3. After the pudding has set, give it a good stir to redistribute the chia seeds and yogurt.
4. Divide the chia seed pudding into serving bowls or jars.
5. Top the pudding with your favorite toppings, such as fresh berries, sliced fruit, nuts, seeds, shredded coconut, or an extra drizzle of honey or maple syrup if desired.
6. Serve the protein-packed chia seed pudding with Greek yogurt chilled and enjoy!

This protein-packed chia seed pudding with Greek yogurt is a nutritious and delicious breakfast, snack, or dessert option. It's rich in fiber, omega-3 fatty acids, and protein, making it a satisfying and wholesome treat. Feel free to customize the recipe with your favorite flavors and toppings to suit your taste preferences!

Breakfast Quinoa Bowl with Almonds and Honey

Ingredients:

- 1/2 cup quinoa, rinsed
- 1 cup water or milk (dairy or non-dairy)
- 1/4 teaspoon ground cinnamon
- 1/4 teaspoon vanilla extract
- Pinch of salt
- 2 tablespoons sliced almonds
- 1 tablespoon honey or maple syrup
- Optional toppings: fresh berries, sliced fruit, yogurt, shredded coconut

Instructions:

1. In a small saucepan, combine the quinoa, water or milk, ground cinnamon, vanilla extract, and salt. Bring to a boil over medium heat.
2. Reduce the heat to low, cover, and simmer for 15-20 minutes, or until the quinoa is cooked and the liquid is absorbed.
3. Fluff the quinoa with a fork and divide it between serving bowls.
4. Top each bowl of quinoa with sliced almonds and drizzle with honey or maple syrup.
5. Add any optional toppings you like, such as fresh berries, sliced fruit, yogurt, or shredded coconut.
6. Serve the breakfast quinoa bowls warm and enjoy!

This breakfast quinoa bowl with almonds and honey is a nutritious and satisfying way to start your day. It's packed with protein, fiber, and healthy fats, and can be customized with your favorite toppings to suit your taste preferences. Enjoy it as a delicious and wholesome breakfast option!

Turkey and Egg Breakfast Sandwich

Ingredients:

- 2 slices of your favorite bread (such as whole grain, sourdough, or English muffin)
- 2 large eggs
- 2 slices of turkey breast (or deli turkey)
- 2 slices of cheese (such as cheddar, Swiss, or American)
- Butter or cooking spray
- Salt and pepper, to taste
- Optional toppings: lettuce, tomato, avocado, sliced red onion, mayonnaise, mustard

Instructions:

1. Heat a non-stick skillet over medium heat. Add a little butter or cooking spray to the skillet.
2. Crack the eggs into the skillet and season with salt and pepper to taste. Cook the eggs to your desired doneness, either fried, scrambled, or as a folded omelette.
3. While the eggs are cooking, toast the slices of bread until golden brown.
4. Once the eggs are cooked, remove them from the skillet and set aside.
5. In the same skillet, add the turkey slices and cook for 1-2 minutes on each side, or until heated through.
6. Place a slice of cheese on top of each turkey slice and let it melt slightly.
7. Assemble the sandwich by placing one slice of bread on a plate. Top with the cooked turkey and melted cheese, followed by the cooked eggs.
8. Add any optional toppings you like, such as lettuce, tomato, avocado, sliced red onion, mayonnaise, or mustard.
9. Place the second slice of bread on top to form a sandwich.
10. Slice the sandwich in half if desired, and serve immediately.

This turkey and egg breakfast sandwich is a delicious and satisfying way to start your day. It's packed with protein, vitamins, and minerals, and can be customized with your favorite toppings to suit your taste preferences. Enjoy it for breakfast, brunch, or any time of day!

Protein-Packed Banana Bread with Whey Protein Powder

Ingredients:

- 1 1/2 cups mashed ripe bananas (about 3-4 medium bananas)
- 1/2 cup plain Greek yogurt
- 1/4 cup honey or maple syrup
- 2 large eggs
- 1 teaspoon vanilla extract
- 1 1/2 cups whole wheat flour or all-purpose flour
- 1/2 cup whey protein powder
- 1 teaspoon baking soda
- 1/2 teaspoon baking powder
- 1/2 teaspoon ground cinnamon
- 1/4 teaspoon salt
- Optional mix-ins: chopped nuts, chocolate chips, dried fruit

Instructions:

1. Preheat your oven to 350°F (175°C). Grease a 9x5-inch loaf pan with cooking spray or butter.
2. In a large mixing bowl, combine the mashed bananas, Greek yogurt, honey or maple syrup, eggs, and vanilla extract. Mix until well combined.
3. In a separate bowl, whisk together the whole wheat flour, whey protein powder, baking soda, baking powder, cinnamon, and salt.
4. Gradually add the dry ingredients to the wet ingredients, stirring until just combined. Be careful not to overmix; a few lumps in the batter are okay.
5. If desired, fold in any optional mix-ins such as chopped nuts, chocolate chips, or dried fruit.
6. Pour the batter into the prepared loaf pan and smooth the top with a spatula.
7. Bake in the preheated oven for 50-60 minutes, or until a toothpick inserted into the center comes out clean.
8. Remove the banana bread from the oven and let it cool in the pan for 10 minutes.
9. Carefully transfer the banana bread to a wire rack to cool completely before slicing.
10. Slice the protein-packed banana bread and serve it plain or with your favorite toppings.

This protein-packed banana bread with whey protein powder is a delicious and nutritious treat that's perfect for breakfast, snack, or dessert. It's moist, tender, and packed with protein, making it a satisfying and wholesome option. Enjoy it on its own or with a spread of nut butter or Greek yogurt for an extra protein boost!

High-Protein Breakfast Wrap with Chicken and Vegetables

Ingredients:

- 1 large whole wheat or spinach tortilla
- 1 cooked chicken breast, sliced or shredded
- 2 large eggs
- 1/4 cup diced bell peppers (any color)
- 1/4 cup diced tomatoes
- 1/4 cup diced onions
- 1/4 cup shredded cheese (such as cheddar or mozzarella)
- 1 tablespoon olive oil or cooking oil of your choice
- Salt and pepper, to taste
- Optional toppings: avocado slices, salsa, hot sauce, Greek yogurt or sour cream

Instructions:

1. In a small skillet, heat the olive oil over medium heat. Add the diced bell peppers, tomatoes, and onions to the skillet. Cook for 3-4 minutes, or until softened.
2. Push the cooked vegetables to one side of the skillet and crack the eggs into the empty side. Season the eggs with salt and pepper, then scramble them until cooked through.
3. Lay the whole wheat or spinach tortilla flat on a plate or cutting board.
4. Place the cooked chicken breast slices or shredded chicken in the center of the tortilla.
5. Spoon the cooked vegetables and scrambled eggs on top of the chicken.
6. Sprinkle the shredded cheese over the vegetables and eggs.
7. Fold the sides of the tortilla over the filling, then roll it up tightly from the bottom to form a wrap.
8. Optional: If desired, heat a clean skillet over medium heat and lightly toast the wrapped breakfast wrap on both sides until golden brown and the cheese is melted.
9. Remove the breakfast wrap from the skillet and slice it in half diagonally.
10. Serve the high-protein breakfast wrap with optional toppings such as avocado slices, salsa, hot sauce, or Greek yogurt or sour cream.

This high-protein breakfast wrap with chicken and vegetables is a nutritious and satisfying meal that's perfect for starting your day on the right foot. It's packed with protein, fiber, vitamins, and minerals, and can be customized with your favorite vegetables and toppings to suit your taste preferences. Enjoy it as a delicious and convenient breakfast option!

Chocolate Protein Overnight Oats with Almond Milk

Ingredients:

- 1/2 cup rolled oats
- 1 tablespoon chia seeds
- 1 scoop chocolate protein powder
- 1 tablespoon unsweetened cocoa powder
- 1/2 cup almond milk (or any milk of your choice)
- 1 tablespoon maple syrup or honey (optional, for sweetness)
- 1/2 teaspoon vanilla extract
- Optional toppings: sliced bananas, berries, nuts, shredded coconut, chocolate chips

Instructions:

1. In a mason jar or airtight container, combine the rolled oats, chia seeds, chocolate protein powder, and unsweetened cocoa powder.
2. Pour in the almond milk, maple syrup or honey (if using), and vanilla extract.
3. Stir the ingredients together until well combined and there are no clumps of protein powder or cocoa powder.
4. Seal the jar or container tightly and refrigerate overnight, or for at least 4 hours, to allow the oats and chia seeds to absorb the liquid and soften.
5. The next morning, give the overnight oats a good stir. If the mixture is too thick, you can add a little more almond milk to reach your desired consistency.
6. Taste the overnight oats and adjust the sweetness if needed by adding more maple syrup or honey.
7. Serve the chocolate protein overnight oats chilled, straight from the refrigerator, or warm them up in the microwave for 30-60 seconds if you prefer.
8. Top the overnight oats with your favorite toppings, such as sliced bananas, berries, nuts, shredded coconut, or chocolate chips.
9. Enjoy your delicious and nutritious chocolate protein overnight oats as a convenient and satisfying breakfast option!

This recipe is customizable, so feel free to adjust the ingredients and toppings to suit your taste preferences. Whether you enjoy them cold or warm, these chocolate protein overnight oats are sure to fuel your day with protein, fiber, and energy!

Egg White Breakfast Burrito with Black Beans and Salsa

Ingredients:

- 2 large egg whites
- 1 whole wheat or spinach tortilla
- 1/4 cup canned black beans, drained and rinsed
- 2 tablespoons salsa (store-bought or homemade)
- 1 tablespoon chopped fresh cilantro (optional)
- Salt and pepper, to taste
- Cooking spray or olive oil

Instructions:

1. Heat a non-stick skillet over medium heat and lightly coat it with cooking spray or olive oil.
2. In a small bowl, season the egg whites with salt and pepper to taste and whisk until frothy.
3. Pour the seasoned egg whites into the skillet and cook, stirring occasionally, until they are set and scrambled.
4. Warm the whole wheat or spinach tortilla in the microwave or on a separate skillet for a few seconds to make it pliable.
5. Once the egg whites are cooked, transfer them to the center of the tortilla.
6. Spoon the black beans and salsa over the egg whites.
7. Sprinkle the chopped fresh cilantro over the top, if using.
8. Fold the sides of the tortilla over the filling, then roll it up tightly from the bottom to form a burrito.
9. Optional: If desired, you can lightly toast the assembled burrito in a clean skillet over medium heat for a minute or two on each side until golden brown and crispy.
10. Serve the egg white breakfast burrito immediately, whole or sliced in half, and enjoy!

This egg white breakfast burrito with black beans and salsa is a delicious and nutritious way to start your day. It's packed with protein, fiber, and flavor, and can be customized with your favorite toppings such as avocado, cheese, or hot sauce. Enjoy it for breakfast, brunch, or any time of day!

Protein-Packed Breakfast Casserole with Turkey Bacon and Cheese

Ingredients:

- 8 slices turkey bacon, chopped
- 8 large eggs
- 1 cup milk (dairy or non-dairy)
- 1 teaspoon Dijon mustard
- Salt and pepper, to taste
- 2 cups shredded cheese (such as cheddar, mozzarella, or Swiss)
- 4 cups cubed bread (such as whole grain, sourdough, or French bread)
- 1/2 cup diced bell peppers (any color)
- 1/2 cup diced onions
- Cooking spray or olive oil

Instructions:

1. Preheat your oven to 350°F (175°C). Grease a 9x13-inch baking dish with cooking spray or olive oil.
2. In a large skillet, cook the chopped turkey bacon over medium heat until crispy. Remove the cooked bacon from the skillet and drain on paper towels.
3. In a large mixing bowl, whisk together the eggs, milk, Dijon mustard, salt, and pepper until well combined.
4. Stir in the shredded cheese, cubed bread, cooked turkey bacon, diced bell peppers, and diced onions until everything is evenly coated with the egg mixture.
5. Pour the mixture into the prepared baking dish, spreading it out evenly.
6. Cover the baking dish with aluminum foil and bake in the preheated oven for 30 minutes.
7. Remove the foil and continue baking for an additional 15-20 minutes, or until the casserole is set and the top is golden brown and crispy.
8. Remove the breakfast casserole from the oven and let it cool for a few minutes before slicing and serving.
9. Serve the protein-packed breakfast casserole with turkey bacon and cheese warm, garnished with chopped fresh herbs if desired.

This protein-packed breakfast casserole with turkey bacon and cheese is a delicious and satisfying meal that's perfect for feeding a crowd or meal prep. It's loaded with protein, vitamins, and minerals, and can be customized with your favorite vegetables or spices to suit your taste preferences. Enjoy it for breakfast, brunch, or any time of day!

Peanut Butter Protein Balls with Rolled Oats and Honey

Ingredients:

- 1 cup rolled oats
- 1/2 cup natural peanut butter (creamy or crunchy)
- 1/4 cup honey or maple syrup
- 1/4 cup protein powder (vanilla or chocolate flavor)
- 1/4 cup mini chocolate chips (optional)
- 1 teaspoon vanilla extract
- Pinch of salt (optional)

Instructions:

1. In a large mixing bowl, combine the rolled oats, peanut butter, honey or maple syrup, protein powder, mini chocolate chips (if using), vanilla extract, and a pinch of salt (if desired).
2. Stir the ingredients together until well combined. If the mixture seems too dry, you can add a little more peanut butter or honey to help it stick together.
3. Once the mixture is well combined, use your hands to roll it into small balls, about 1 inch in diameter, and place them on a baking sheet lined with parchment paper.
4. Repeat until all of the mixture has been rolled into balls.
5. Place the baking sheet in the refrigerator for at least 30 minutes to allow the protein balls to firm up.
6. Once firm, transfer the peanut butter protein balls to an airtight container and store them in the refrigerator for up to one week.
7. Enjoy the peanut butter protein balls as a nutritious and satisfying snack any time of day!

These peanut butter protein balls with rolled oats and honey are packed with protein, fiber, and healthy fats, making them a perfect on-the-go snack or post-workout treat.

Feel free to customize the recipe by adding your favorite mix-ins such as chopped nuts, dried fruit, or shredded coconut. Enjoy!

Protein-Packed Green Smoothie with Kale and Hemp Seeds

Ingredients:

- 1 cup kale leaves, stems removed
- 1 ripe banana, peeled and sliced
- 1/2 cup plain Greek yogurt
- 1 tablespoon hemp seeds
- 1 tablespoon almond butter or peanut butter
- 1/2 cup unsweetened almond milk (or any milk of your choice)
- 1/2 cup ice cubes
- Optional sweetener: honey, maple syrup, or dates (if desired)

Instructions:

1. Place the kale leaves, sliced banana, Greek yogurt, hemp seeds, almond butter or peanut butter, and unsweetened almond milk in a blender.
2. Add the ice cubes to the blender.
3. If you prefer a sweeter smoothie, you can add a drizzle of honey, maple syrup, or a couple of pitted dates to the blender.
4. Blend all the ingredients until smooth and creamy. If the smoothie is too thick, you can add more almond milk until you reach your desired consistency.
5. Pour the protein-packed green smoothie into glasses and serve immediately.
6. Optionally, you can sprinkle additional hemp seeds on top for extra texture and nutrition.

This protein-packed green smoothie with kale and hemp seeds is a delicious and nutritious way to start your day or refuel after a workout. It's packed with protein, fiber, vitamins, and minerals, and the combination of kale, banana, and nut butter creates a creamy and satisfying texture. Enjoy it as a quick and easy breakfast or snack!

Baked Eggs in Avocado with Bacon

Ingredients:

- 2 ripe avocados
- 4 large eggs
- 4 slices of bacon
- Salt and pepper, to taste
- Optional toppings: chopped fresh herbs (such as parsley or chives), hot sauce, salsa

Instructions:

1. Preheat your oven to 425°F (220°C). Line a baking sheet with parchment paper or aluminum foil.
2. Cut the avocados in half lengthwise and remove the pits. Use a spoon to scoop out a little extra flesh from each avocado half to create a larger cavity for the eggs.
3. Place the avocado halves on the prepared baking sheet, cut side up, and gently press them down to create a stable base.
4. Crack one egg into each avocado half, being careful not to overflow the cavity. If the eggs are too large, you can scoop out a little more avocado to make room.
5. Season the eggs with salt and pepper to taste.
6. Cut each slice of bacon in half lengthwise, then wrap each avocado half with two strips of bacon, securing them around the avocado with toothpicks if needed.
7. Place the baking sheet in the preheated oven and bake for 15-20 minutes, or until the eggs reach your desired level of doneness and the bacon is crispy.
8. Remove the baked eggs in avocado with bacon from the oven and let them cool for a few minutes before serving.
9. Garnish the baked eggs with optional toppings such as chopped fresh herbs, hot sauce, or salsa.
10. Serve the baked eggs in avocado with bacon warm and enjoy!

This recipe is a delicious and nutritious twist on classic baked eggs, with creamy avocado and crispy bacon adding extra flavor and texture. It's a satisfying and filling breakfast or brunch option that's sure to impress!

Protein-Packed Breakfast Bagel with Cream Cheese and Smoked Salmon

Ingredients:

- 1 whole grain or everything bagel, sliced and toasted
- 2 tablespoons cream cheese (plain or flavored)
- 2 ounces smoked salmon
- 1 tablespoon capers, drained
- Sliced red onion (optional)
- Fresh dill, chopped (optional)
- Lemon wedges (optional)
- Salt and pepper, to taste

Instructions:

1. Toast the sliced bagel halves until golden brown.
2. Spread a tablespoon of cream cheese on each half of the toasted bagel.
3. Top each bagel half with slices of smoked salmon.
4. Sprinkle capers evenly over the smoked salmon.
5. If desired, add a few slices of red onion on top for extra flavor.
6. Garnish with chopped fresh dill, if using.
7. Squeeze a lemon wedge over the top of each bagel half, if desired, and season with salt and pepper to taste.
8. Serve the protein-packed breakfast bagel immediately and enjoy!

This protein-packed breakfast bagel with cream cheese and smoked salmon is a delicious and satisfying way to start your day. It's packed with protein, healthy fats, and flavor, and the combination of creamy cream cheese, savory smoked salmon, and tangy capers is simply irresistible. Enjoy it for breakfast, brunch, or as a light lunch option!

Quinoa Protein Pancakes with Cottage Cheese

Ingredients:

- 1 cup cooked quinoa, cooled
- 1/2 cup cottage cheese
- 2 large eggs
- 1/4 cup milk (dairy or non-dairy)
- 1 tablespoon honey or maple syrup
- 1 teaspoon vanilla extract
- 1/2 cup whole wheat flour or all-purpose flour
- 1 teaspoon baking powder
- Pinch of salt
- Cooking spray or butter, for greasing the skillet
- Optional toppings: fresh berries, sliced bananas, Greek yogurt, maple syrup

Instructions:

1. In a blender or food processor, combine the cooked quinoa, cottage cheese, eggs, milk, honey or maple syrup, and vanilla extract. Blend until smooth.
2. In a large mixing bowl, whisk together the whole wheat flour or all-purpose flour, baking powder, and a pinch of salt.
3. Pour the quinoa mixture from the blender into the bowl with the dry ingredients. Stir until just combined. Be careful not to overmix; a few lumps in the batter are okay.
4. Heat a non-stick skillet or griddle over medium heat. Lightly grease the skillet with cooking spray or butter.
5. Pour about 1/4 cup of batter onto the skillet for each pancake, spreading it out slightly with the back of a spoon if needed.
6. Cook the pancakes for 2-3 minutes, or until bubbles form on the surface and the edges start to look set.
7. Flip the pancakes and cook for an additional 1-2 minutes on the other side, or until golden brown and cooked through.
8. Remove the pancakes from the skillet and keep them warm while you cook the remaining batter.

9. Serve the quinoa protein pancakes with cottage cheese warm, topped with your favorite toppings such as fresh berries, sliced bananas, Greek yogurt, or maple syrup.
10. Enjoy these nutritious and delicious pancakes for breakfast or brunch!

These quinoa protein pancakes with cottage cheese are a nutritious and satisfying breakfast option that's packed with protein, fiber, and flavor. They're easy to make and can be customized with your favorite toppings to suit your taste preferences. Enjoy them as a wholesome start to your day!

Breakfast Power Bowl with Sweet Potato and Black Beans

Ingredients:

For the bowl:

- 1 large sweet potato, diced into cubes
- 1 tablespoon olive oil
- 1 teaspoon ground cumin
- 1 teaspoon paprika
- Salt and pepper, to taste
- 1 cup cooked quinoa or brown rice
- 1 cup cooked black beans (canned or homemade)
- 2 cups baby spinach or kale, chopped
- 2 large eggs
- Optional toppings: sliced avocado, salsa, chopped fresh cilantro, lime wedges

For the dressing (optional):

- 2 tablespoons plain Greek yogurt
- 1 tablespoon lime juice
- 1 tablespoon chopped fresh cilantro
- 1/2 teaspoon ground cumin
- Salt and pepper, to taste

Instructions:

1. Preheat your oven to 400°F (200°C).
2. In a large bowl, toss the diced sweet potato with olive oil, ground cumin, paprika, salt, and pepper until evenly coated.
3. Spread the seasoned sweet potato cubes in a single layer on a baking sheet lined with parchment paper.
4. Roast the sweet potato in the preheated oven for 25-30 minutes, or until tender and lightly browned, stirring halfway through cooking.

5. While the sweet potato is roasting, prepare the optional dressing by whisking together the plain Greek yogurt, lime juice, chopped fresh cilantro, ground cumin, salt, and pepper in a small bowl. Set aside.
6. In a separate skillet, heat a little olive oil over medium heat. Add the cooked quinoa or brown rice and black beans, stirring occasionally until heated through.
7. Add the chopped baby spinach or kale to the skillet with the quinoa and black beans, stirring until wilted.
8. In another skillet, cook the eggs to your desired doneness (fried, scrambled, or poached).
9. To assemble the breakfast power bowls, divide the quinoa, black bean, and spinach mixture among serving bowls. Top each bowl with roasted sweet potato cubes and a cooked egg.
10. Drizzle the optional dressing over the top of each bowl, if desired.
11. Garnish the breakfast power bowls with optional toppings such as sliced avocado, salsa, chopped fresh cilantro, and lime wedges.
12. Serve the breakfast power bowls warm and enjoy!

These breakfast power bowls with sweet potato and black beans are packed with protein, fiber, vitamins, and minerals, making them a nutritious and satisfying meal to start your day. They're versatile and customizable, so feel free to adjust the ingredients and toppings to suit your taste preferences. Enjoy!

High-Protein Banana Nut Muffins with Greek Yogurt

Ingredients:

- 2 ripe bananas, mashed
- 1/2 cup plain Greek yogurt
- 1/4 cup honey or maple syrup
- 2 large eggs
- 1 teaspoon vanilla extract
- 1 1/2 cups whole wheat flour or all-purpose flour
- 1/2 cup vanilla or plain protein powder
- 1 teaspoon baking powder
- 1/2 teaspoon baking soda
- 1/2 teaspoon ground cinnamon
- 1/4 teaspoon salt
- 1/2 cup chopped nuts (such as walnuts or pecans)
- Optional: additional banana slices and nuts for topping

Instructions:

1. Preheat your oven to 350°F (175°C). Line a muffin tin with paper liners or grease with cooking spray.
2. In a large mixing bowl, combine the mashed bananas, Greek yogurt, honey or maple syrup, eggs, and vanilla extract. Mix until well combined.
3. In a separate bowl, whisk together the whole wheat flour or all-purpose flour, protein powder, baking powder, baking soda, ground cinnamon, and salt.
4. Gradually add the dry ingredients to the wet ingredients, stirring until just combined. Be careful not to overmix; a few lumps in the batter are okay.
5. Gently fold in the chopped nuts until evenly distributed throughout the batter.
6. Divide the batter evenly among the muffin cups, filling each about 3/4 full.
7. If desired, top each muffin with a slice of banana and a sprinkle of chopped nuts for garnish.
8. Bake in the preheated oven for 18-20 minutes, or until a toothpick inserted into the center of a muffin comes out clean.
9. Remove the muffins from the oven and let them cool in the tin for a few minutes before transferring them to a wire rack to cool completely.

10. Once cooled, store the high-protein banana nut muffins in an airtight container at room temperature for up to 3 days, or in the refrigerator for up to 1 week.
11. Enjoy these delicious and nutritious muffins for a high-protein breakfast or snack!

These high-protein banana nut muffins with Greek yogurt are moist, flavorful, and packed with protein, making them a perfect on-the-go breakfast or snack option. They're easy to make and can be enjoyed fresh out of the oven or stored for later. Feel free to customize the recipe with your favorite nuts or add-ins for a delicious twist!

Protein-Packed Breakfast Tacos with Egg and Beans

Ingredients:

- 4 small flour or corn tortillas
- 4 large eggs
- 1 tablespoon olive oil
- 1/2 cup cooked black beans (canned or homemade), drained and rinsed
- Salt and pepper, to taste
- Optional toppings: diced avocado, salsa, chopped fresh cilantro, shredded cheese, hot sauce

Instructions:

1. Warm the tortillas in a dry skillet over medium heat for about 30 seconds on each side, or until heated through. Alternatively, you can wrap the tortillas in a damp paper towel and microwave them for 30-60 seconds.
2. In a separate skillet, heat the olive oil over medium heat.
3. Crack the eggs into the skillet and cook to your desired doneness (fried, scrambled, or poached). Season with salt and pepper to taste.
4. While the eggs are cooking, warm the black beans in a small saucepan over low heat or in the microwave.
5. Once the eggs are cooked, assemble the breakfast tacos by placing a spoonful of black beans on each warm tortilla.
6. Top the black beans with the cooked eggs.
7. Add any optional toppings you like, such as diced avocado, salsa, chopped fresh cilantro, shredded cheese, or hot sauce.
8. Serve the protein-packed breakfast tacos immediately and enjoy!

These protein-packed breakfast tacos with egg and beans are a delicious and satisfying way to start your day. They're loaded with protein, fiber, and flavor, and the customizable toppings make them perfect for adding your favorite flavors. Enjoy them for breakfast, brunch, or any time of day!

Blueberry Protein Muffins with Whey Protein Powder

Ingredients:

- 1 1/2 cups whole wheat flour or all-purpose flour
- 1/2 cup vanilla whey protein powder
- 1 teaspoon baking powder
- 1/2 teaspoon baking soda
- 1/4 teaspoon salt
- 1/2 cup unsweetened applesauce
- 1/4 cup honey or maple syrup
- 1/4 cup plain Greek yogurt
- 2 large eggs
- 1 teaspoon vanilla extract
- 1 cup fresh or frozen blueberries

Instructions:

1. Preheat your oven to 350°F (175°C). Grease a muffin tin or line it with muffin liners.
2. In a large mixing bowl, whisk together the flour, protein powder, baking powder, baking soda, and salt.
3. In a separate bowl, mix together the applesauce, honey or maple syrup, Greek yogurt, eggs, and vanilla extract until well combined.
4. Pour the wet ingredients into the dry ingredients and stir until just combined. Be careful not to overmix; a few lumps in the batter are okay.
5. Gently fold in the blueberries until evenly distributed throughout the batter.
6. Divide the batter evenly among the muffin cups, filling each about 3/4 full.
7. Bake in the preheated oven for 18-20 minutes, or until a toothpick inserted into the center of a muffin comes out clean.
8. Remove the muffins from the oven and let them cool in the tin for a few minutes before transferring them to a wire rack to cool completely.
9. Enjoy these delicious and nutritious blueberry protein muffins as a convenient breakfast or snack!

These blueberry protein muffins are packed with protein from the whey protein powder and Greek yogurt, making them a satisfying and wholesome option for breakfast or snack time. They're moist, flavorful, and bursting with juicy blueberries. Enjoy them fresh out of the oven or store them in an airtight container for later!

Veggie and Tofu Breakfast Stir-Fry

Ingredients:

- 14 oz (400g) firm tofu, drained and pressed
- 2 tablespoons soy sauce (or tamari for gluten-free)
- 1 tablespoon sesame oil
- 1 tablespoon olive oil or vegetable oil
- 2 cloves garlic, minced
- 1 teaspoon grated ginger
- 1 bell pepper, thinly sliced
- 1 cup sliced mushrooms
- 1 cup broccoli florets
- 1 cup spinach leaves
- Salt and pepper, to taste
- Optional toppings: sliced green onions, sesame seeds

Instructions:

1. Cut the pressed tofu into cubes.
2. In a small bowl, mix together the soy sauce and sesame oil. Add the tofu cubes to the bowl and gently toss to coat. Let the tofu marinate for about 10-15 minutes.
3. Heat the olive oil or vegetable oil in a large skillet or wok over medium-high heat.
4. Add the minced garlic and grated ginger to the skillet and cook for about 1 minute, or until fragrant.
5. Add the marinated tofu cubes to the skillet, spreading them out in a single layer. Cook for 5-7 minutes, stirring occasionally, until the tofu is golden brown and crispy on all sides. Remove the tofu from the skillet and set aside.
6. In the same skillet, add the sliced bell pepper, mushrooms, and broccoli florets. Cook for 5-7 minutes, or until the vegetables are tender-crisp.
7. Add the spinach leaves to the skillet and cook for an additional 1-2 minutes, or until wilted.
8. Return the cooked tofu to the skillet and toss everything together until well combined. Season with salt and pepper to taste.
9. Serve the veggie and tofu breakfast stir-fry hot, garnished with sliced green onions and sesame seeds if desired.

10. Enjoy this flavorful and nutritious stir-fry as a delicious breakfast option!

This veggie and tofu breakfast stir-fry is packed with protein, vitamins, and minerals, making it a wholesome and satisfying way to start your day. It's quick and easy to make, and you can customize it with your favorite vegetables and toppings. Enjoy!

Protein-Packed French Toast with Whole Wheat Bread

Ingredients:

- 4 slices of whole wheat bread
- 4 large eggs
- 1/2 cup milk (dairy or non-dairy)
- 1 scoop of your favorite protein powder (vanilla or chocolate flavor)
- 1 teaspoon vanilla extract
- 1/2 teaspoon ground cinnamon
- Cooking spray or butter, for greasing the skillet
- Optional toppings: fresh berries, sliced bananas, Greek yogurt, maple syrup

Instructions:

1. In a shallow dish or bowl, whisk together the eggs, milk, protein powder, vanilla extract, and ground cinnamon until well combined.
2. Heat a non-stick skillet or griddle over medium heat and lightly grease it with cooking spray or butter.
3. Dip each slice of whole wheat bread into the egg mixture, making sure to coat both sides evenly.
4. Place the coated bread slices onto the preheated skillet or griddle. Cook for 2-3 minutes on each side, or until golden brown and cooked through.
5. Repeat the process with the remaining slices of bread, adding more cooking spray or butter to the skillet or griddle as needed.
6. Once all the French toast slices are cooked, transfer them to serving plates.
7. Serve the protein-packed French toast warm, topped with your favorite toppings such as fresh berries, sliced bananas, Greek yogurt, or maple syrup.
8. Enjoy this delicious and nutritious breakfast option!

This protein-packed French toast with whole wheat bread is a satisfying and wholesome way to start your day. It's packed with protein, fiber, and flavor, and the customizable toppings make it perfect for adding your favorite flavors. Enjoy it for breakfast, brunch, or any time of day!

Protein Oat Bars with Almond Butter and Protein Powder

Ingredients:

- 2 cups rolled oats
- 1/2 cup protein powder (vanilla or chocolate flavor)
- 1/2 cup almond butter
- 1/4 cup honey or maple syrup
- 1/4 cup almond milk (or any milk of your choice)
- 1 teaspoon vanilla extract
- 1/2 teaspoon ground cinnamon (optional)
- Pinch of salt

Optional add-ins:

- 1/4 cup chopped nuts (such as almonds, walnuts, or pecans)
- 1/4 cup dried fruit (such as raisins, cranberries, or chopped apricots)
- 1/4 cup chocolate chips

Instructions:

1. Preheat your oven to 350°F (175°C). Grease an 8x8-inch baking dish or line it with parchment paper.
2. In a large mixing bowl, combine the rolled oats, protein powder, and optional ground cinnamon. Stir until well combined.
3. In a small saucepan, heat the almond butter, honey or maple syrup, almond milk, vanilla extract, and a pinch of salt over low heat. Stir constantly until the mixture is smooth and well combined.
4. Pour the almond butter mixture over the dry ingredients in the mixing bowl. Stir until the oats are evenly coated and the mixture starts to come together. If the mixture seems too dry, you can add a little more almond milk.
5. Fold in any optional add-ins such as chopped nuts, dried fruit, or chocolate chips.
6. Press the mixture firmly and evenly into the prepared baking dish.
7. Bake in the preheated oven for 15-20 minutes, or until the edges are golden brown and the bars are set.
8. Remove the baking dish from the oven and let the bars cool completely in the dish.

9. Once cooled, use a sharp knife to cut the bars into squares or rectangles.
10. Store the protein oat bars in an airtight container at room temperature for up to one week, or in the refrigerator for longer freshness.
11. Enjoy these protein oat bars as a convenient and nutritious snack or breakfast option!

These protein oat bars with almond butter and protein powder are packed with protein, fiber, and flavor, making them a perfect on-the-go snack or breakfast option. They're easy to make and can be customized with your favorite add-ins to suit your taste preferences. Enjoy!

Breakfast Egg Cups with Ham and Cheese

Ingredients:

- 6 large eggs
- 1/4 cup milk (dairy or non-dairy)
- Salt and pepper, to taste
- 1 cup diced cooked ham
- 1/2 cup shredded cheese (such as cheddar, mozzarella, or Swiss)
- Optional add-ins: diced bell peppers, diced onions, chopped spinach, diced tomatoes

Instructions:

1. Preheat your oven to 350°F (175°C). Grease a muffin tin with cooking spray or line it with silicone muffin liners.
2. In a mixing bowl, whisk together the eggs, milk, salt, and pepper until well combined.
3. Divide the diced ham evenly among the muffin cups, filling each about halfway.
4. Sprinkle the shredded cheese over the ham in each muffin cup.
5. If using any optional add-ins, distribute them evenly among the muffin cups.
6. Pour the egg mixture over the ham, cheese, and optional add-ins in each muffin cup, filling them almost to the top.
7. Gently stir the contents of each muffin cup to ensure that the egg mixture is evenly distributed.
8. Bake in the preheated oven for 18-20 minutes, or until the egg cups are set and the tops are lightly golden brown.
9. Remove the muffin tin from the oven and let the egg cups cool for a few minutes before removing them from the muffin tin.
10. Serve the breakfast egg cups warm and enjoy!

These breakfast egg cups with ham and cheese are a convenient and portable breakfast option that's packed with protein and flavor. They're easy to make and can be customized with your favorite ingredients. Enjoy them for a quick and satisfying breakfast on busy mornings!

Protein-Packed Breakfast Pizza with Egg and Turkey Bacon

Ingredients:

- 1 pre-made whole wheat pizza crust (or homemade if preferred)
- 1 tablespoon olive oil
- 4 large eggs
- 4 slices turkey bacon, cooked and chopped
- 1 cup shredded cheese (such as mozzarella or cheddar)
- Salt and pepper, to taste
- Optional toppings: diced bell peppers, sliced mushrooms, diced tomatoes, chopped spinach

Instructions:

1. Preheat your oven to the temperature specified on the pizza crust package (usually around 400°F or 200°C).
2. If your pizza crust is not pre-cooked, follow the package instructions to pre-bake it for a few minutes before adding the toppings.
3. While the crust is pre-baking, heat the olive oil in a skillet over medium heat. Crack the eggs into the skillet and cook to your desired doneness (fried or scrambled). Season with salt and pepper to taste.
4. Once the crust is pre-baked, remove it from the oven and top it with the cooked eggs, chopped turkey bacon, and any optional toppings you like.
5. Sprinkle the shredded cheese evenly over the top of the pizza.
6. Return the pizza to the oven and bake for another 8-10 minutes, or until the cheese is melted and bubbly.
7. Remove the pizza from the oven and let it cool for a few minutes before slicing.
8. Serve the protein-packed breakfast pizza warm and enjoy!

This protein-packed breakfast pizza with egg and turkey bacon is a delicious and satisfying way to start your day. It's loaded with protein and flavor, and you can customize it with your favorite toppings to suit your taste preferences. Enjoy it for breakfast, brunch, or any time of day!

Protein-Packed Breakfast Sushi with Smoked Salmon and Avocado

Ingredients:

- 2 nori seaweed sheets
- 1 cup cooked sushi rice (short-grain rice seasoned with rice vinegar, sugar, and salt)
- 4 ounces smoked salmon, thinly sliced
- 1 ripe avocado, thinly sliced
- 2 tablespoons cream cheese (optional)
- Soy sauce, for dipping
- Wasabi paste, for serving (optional)
- Pickled ginger, for serving (optional)
- Sesame seeds, for garnish (optional)

Instructions:

1. Place a nori seaweed sheet on a bamboo sushi rolling mat or a clean kitchen towel.
2. Spread half of the cooked sushi rice evenly over the nori sheet, leaving a 1-inch border along the top edge.
3. If using, spread a thin layer of cream cheese over the rice on the nori sheet.
4. Arrange half of the smoked salmon slices horizontally across the bottom edge of the nori sheet.
5. Arrange half of the avocado slices next to the smoked salmon.
6. Starting from the bottom edge, tightly roll up the nori sheet with the filling into a sushi roll, using the bamboo sushi rolling mat or kitchen towel to help shape and compress the roll.
7. Repeat the process with the remaining nori sheet and ingredients to make the second sushi roll.
8. Use a sharp knife to slice each sushi roll into 6-8 pieces.
9. Arrange the protein-packed breakfast sushi pieces on a serving platter.
10. Serve the breakfast sushi with soy sauce for dipping and, if desired, wasabi paste and pickled ginger on the side.
11. Optionally, sprinkle sesame seeds over the top of the sushi pieces for garnish.
12. Enjoy your protein-packed breakfast sushi with smoked salmon and avocado!

This protein-packed breakfast sushi with smoked salmon and avocado is a creative and delicious way to enjoy a nutritious breakfast. It's packed with protein, healthy fats, and flavor, making it a satisfying and energizing meal to start your day. Plus, it's fun to make and can be customized with your favorite sushi fillings and toppings. Enjoy!

High-Protein Breakfast Trifle with Greek Yogurt and Granola

Ingredients:

- 2 cups Greek yogurt (plain or flavored)
- 1 cup granola (homemade or store-bought)
- 1 cup mixed fresh berries (such as strawberries, blueberries, raspberries)
- 1 tablespoon honey or maple syrup (optional)
- Fresh mint leaves, for garnish (optional)

Instructions:

1. In a small bowl, mix the Greek yogurt with honey or maple syrup, if using, until well combined.
2. In serving glasses or bowls, layer the ingredients to create the trifle. Start with a layer of Greek yogurt at the bottom of each glass.
3. Add a layer of granola on top of the Greek yogurt, followed by a layer of mixed fresh berries.
4. Repeat the layers until you reach the top of the glasses, finishing with a layer of Greek yogurt on top.
5. Garnish the top of each trifle with additional granola and fresh berries.
6. Optionally, garnish each trifle with a sprig of fresh mint leaves for added freshness and flavor.
7. Serve the high-protein breakfast trifles immediately and enjoy!

This high-protein breakfast trifle with Greek yogurt and granola is a delicious and satisfying way to start your day. It's packed with protein, fiber, and antioxidants from the Greek yogurt and berries, while the granola adds crunch and texture. Plus, it's easy to customize with your favorite toppings and flavors. Enjoy it as a nutritious and energizing breakfast option!

Cottage Cheese and Fruit Bowl with Almonds

Ingredients:

- 1 cup cottage cheese
- 1 cup mixed fresh fruit (such as berries, sliced bananas, diced peaches, or sliced kiwi)
- 2 tablespoons sliced almonds
- Honey or maple syrup (optional, for drizzling)
- Fresh mint leaves (optional, for garnish)

Instructions:

1. Spoon the cottage cheese into a serving bowl or individual bowls.
2. Arrange the mixed fresh fruit on top of the cottage cheese.
3. Sprinkle the sliced almonds over the fruit and cottage cheese.
4. If desired, drizzle honey or maple syrup over the top for a touch of sweetness.
5. Optionally, garnish the bowl(s) with fresh mint leaves for added freshness and flavor.
6. Serve the cottage cheese and fruit bowl with almonds immediately and enjoy!

This cottage cheese and fruit bowl with almonds is a delicious and nutritious breakfast or snack option. It's packed with protein from the cottage cheese and almonds, while the fresh fruit adds natural sweetness and vitamins. Feel free to customize the recipe with your favorite fruits and toppings. Enjoy!

Protein-Packed Breakfast Crepes with Cottage Cheese Filling

Ingredients:

For the crepes:

- 1 cup all-purpose flour
- 2 large eggs
- 1 cup milk (dairy or non-dairy)
- 2 tablespoons melted butter or oil
- 1 tablespoon sugar (optional)
- 1/2 teaspoon vanilla extract
- Pinch of salt

For the cottage cheese filling:

- 1 cup cottage cheese
- 2 tablespoons honey or maple syrup
- 1/2 teaspoon vanilla extract
- Optional toppings: fresh berries, sliced bananas, chopped nuts, additional honey or maple syrup

Instructions:

1. In a mixing bowl, whisk together the flour, eggs, milk, melted butter or oil, sugar (if using), vanilla extract, and salt until smooth. Let the batter rest for about 15-20 minutes.
2. While the batter is resting, prepare the cottage cheese filling. In a separate bowl, mix together the cottage cheese, honey or maple syrup, and vanilla extract until well combined. Set aside.
3. Heat a non-stick skillet or crepe pan over medium heat. Lightly grease the skillet with butter or oil.
4. Pour about 1/4 cup of the crepe batter into the skillet, swirling it around to coat the bottom evenly. Cook for about 1-2 minutes, or until the edges start to lift and the bottom is golden brown.

5. Carefully flip the crepe using a spatula and cook for another 1-2 minutes on the other side, until golden brown. Repeat with the remaining batter.
6. Once all the crepes are cooked, assemble the crepes by spreading a spoonful of the cottage cheese filling onto each crepe and folding or rolling them up.
7. Serve the protein-packed breakfast crepes with cottage cheese filling warm, topped with your favorite toppings such as fresh berries, sliced bananas, chopped nuts, and additional honey or maple syrup.
8. Enjoy these delicious and nutritious breakfast crepes as a satisfying morning meal!

These protein-packed breakfast crepes with cottage cheese filling are a delicious and wholesome way to start your day. They're easy to make and can be customized with your favorite toppings to suit your taste preferences. Enjoy them for breakfast or brunch with family and friends!

Baked Protein Oatmeal with Apples and Cinnamon

Ingredients:

- 2 cups old-fashioned rolled oats
- 1 scoop (about 1/4 cup) vanilla protein powder
- 1 teaspoon baking powder
- 1 teaspoon ground cinnamon
- 1/4 teaspoon salt
- 2 cups unsweetened almond milk (or any milk of your choice)
- 1/4 cup maple syrup or honey
- 2 large eggs
- 2 tablespoons melted coconut oil or butter
- 1 teaspoon vanilla extract
- 2 medium apples, peeled, cored, and diced
- Optional toppings: sliced apples, chopped nuts, Greek yogurt, additional maple syrup

Instructions:

1. Preheat your oven to 350°F (175°C). Grease a 9x9-inch baking dish with cooking spray or butter.
2. In a large mixing bowl, combine the rolled oats, protein powder, baking powder, ground cinnamon, and salt. Stir until well combined.
3. In another bowl, whisk together the almond milk, maple syrup or honey, eggs, melted coconut oil or butter, and vanilla extract until smooth.
4. Pour the wet ingredients into the bowl with the dry ingredients and mix until everything is evenly combined.
5. Gently fold in the diced apples until they are evenly distributed throughout the oatmeal mixture.
6. Pour the mixture into the prepared baking dish and spread it out evenly.
7. Bake in the preheated oven for 35-40 minutes, or until the top is golden brown and the oatmeal is set.
8. Remove the baked oatmeal from the oven and let it cool for a few minutes before slicing and serving.
9. Serve the baked protein oatmeal with apples and cinnamon warm, topped with your favorite toppings such as sliced apples, chopped nuts, Greek yogurt, and additional maple syrup.

10. Enjoy this delicious and nutritious baked oatmeal as a wholesome breakfast option!

This baked protein oatmeal with apples and cinnamon is a comforting and satisfying breakfast that's packed with protein, fiber, and flavor. It's perfect for meal prep and can be enjoyed warm or cold, making it a versatile option for busy mornings. Plus, you can customize it with your favorite toppings to suit your taste preferences. Enjoy!

Egg and Turkey Sausage Breakfast Burrito Bowl

Ingredients:

For the burrito bowl:

- 4 large eggs
- 4 turkey sausage links or patties, cooked and sliced
- 2 cups cooked quinoa or brown rice
- 1 cup black beans, drained and rinsed
- 1 cup diced bell peppers (any color)
- 1 cup diced tomatoes
- 1 avocado, sliced
- Salt and pepper to taste
- Optional toppings: shredded cheese, salsa, sliced jalapeños, chopped cilantro

Instructions:

1. In a skillet over medium heat, scramble the eggs until cooked through. Season with salt and pepper to taste. Set aside.
2. Divide the cooked quinoa or brown rice evenly among serving bowls.
3. Top each bowl with scrambled eggs, sliced turkey sausage, black beans, diced bell peppers, diced tomatoes, and sliced avocado.
4. Optionally, add any additional toppings you desire, such as shredded cheese, salsa, sliced jalapeños, or chopped cilantro.
5. Serve the egg and turkey sausage breakfast burrito bowls immediately and enjoy!

These breakfast burrito bowls are a delicious and nutritious way to start your day.

Packed with protein, fiber, and flavor, they're sure to keep you satisfied until lunchtime.

Plus, they're easy to customize with your favorite toppings, so feel free to get creative and make them your own!

High-Protein Breakfast Shake with Banana and Peanut Butter

Ingredients:

- 1 ripe banana
- 2 tablespoons peanut butter (or any nut butter of your choice)
- 1 scoop of your favorite protein powder (vanilla or chocolate flavor)
- 1 cup unsweetened almond milk (or any milk of your choice)
- 1/2 cup Greek yogurt (plain or flavored)
- 1 tablespoon honey or maple syrup (optional, for added sweetness)
- Ice cubes (optional, for a thicker shake)

Instructions:

1. Peel the ripe banana and break it into chunks.
2. In a blender, combine the banana chunks, peanut butter, protein powder, almond milk, Greek yogurt, and honey or maple syrup (if using).
3. If you prefer a thicker shake, add a handful of ice cubes to the blender.
4. Blend all the ingredients until smooth and creamy. If necessary, scrape down the sides of the blender and blend again to ensure everything is well combined.
5. Once the shake reaches your desired consistency, pour it into a glass.
6. Optionally, garnish the top of the shake with a drizzle of peanut butter or sliced banana for presentation.
7. Serve the high-protein breakfast shake immediately and enjoy!

This high-protein breakfast shake with banana and peanut butter is a delicious and satisfying way to start your day. Packed with protein, healthy fats, and natural sweetness, it's sure to keep you energized and satisfied until your next meal. Plus, it's quick and easy to make, so you can enjoy it even on busy mornings!

Protein-Packed Breakfast Bars with Quinoa and Nuts

Ingredients:

- 1 cup cooked quinoa, cooled
- 1 cup rolled oats
- 1/2 cup chopped nuts (such as almonds, walnuts, or pecans)
- 1/4 cup dried fruit (such as raisins, cranberries, or chopped apricots)
- 1/4 cup seeds (such as pumpkin seeds or sunflower seeds)
- 1/4 cup honey or maple syrup
- 1/4 cup almond butter or peanut butter
- 1 teaspoon vanilla extract
- 1/2 teaspoon ground cinnamon
- Pinch of salt

Instructions:

1. Preheat your oven to 350°F (175°C). Line an 8x8-inch baking dish with parchment paper, leaving some overhang on the sides for easy removal.
2. In a large mixing bowl, combine the cooked quinoa, rolled oats, chopped nuts, dried fruit, and seeds. Stir until well combined.
3. In a small saucepan, heat the honey or maple syrup, almond butter or peanut butter, vanilla extract, ground cinnamon, and a pinch of salt over low heat. Stir until the mixture is smooth and well combined.
4. Pour the honey or maple syrup mixture over the dry ingredients in the mixing bowl. Stir until all the ingredients are evenly coated.
5. Transfer the mixture to the prepared baking dish and press it down firmly into an even layer.
6. Bake in the preheated oven for 20-25 minutes, or until the edges are golden brown.
7. Remove the baking dish from the oven and let the bars cool completely in the dish.
8. Once cooled, use the parchment paper overhang to lift the bars out of the dish. Place them on a cutting board and slice them into bars or squares.
9. Store the protein-packed breakfast bars in an airtight container at room temperature for up to one week, or in the refrigerator for longer freshness.

10. Enjoy these protein-packed breakfast bars with quinoa and nuts as a convenient and nutritious grab-and-go breakfast or snack!

These protein-packed breakfast bars are loaded with quinoa, nuts, seeds, and dried fruit, making them a wholesome and satisfying option to start your day. They're easy to make and can be customized with your favorite ingredients. Enjoy them as a portable breakfast or snack whenever you need a quick and nutritious boost of energy!

Breakfast Quesadilla with Egg, Cheese, and Black Beans

Ingredients:

- 2 large eggs
- Salt and pepper, to taste
- 2 large flour tortillas
- 1/2 cup shredded cheese (such as cheddar or Monterey Jack)
- 1/4 cup canned black beans, drained and rinsed
- 2 tablespoons diced red onion
- 2 tablespoons chopped fresh cilantro
- Salsa, sour cream, or avocado slices for serving (optional)

Instructions:

1. In a small bowl, whisk together the eggs, salt, and pepper until well combined.
2. Heat a skillet over medium heat and spray it with cooking spray or add a small amount of oil.
3. Pour the beaten eggs into the skillet and scramble them until cooked through. Remove from heat and set aside.
4. Place one flour tortilla in the skillet over medium heat. Sprinkle half of the shredded cheese evenly over the tortilla.
5. Spread the cooked scrambled eggs, black beans, diced red onion, and chopped cilantro evenly over the cheese.
6. Sprinkle the remaining shredded cheese over the toppings.
7. Place the second flour tortilla on top to form a quesadilla. Press down gently with a spatula.
8. Cook the quesadilla for 2-3 minutes on each side, or until golden brown and crispy, and the cheese is melted.
9. Remove the quesadilla from the skillet and let it cool for a minute before slicing it into wedges.
10. Serve the breakfast quesadilla with salsa, sour cream, or avocado slices on the side, if desired.
11. Enjoy your delicious breakfast quesadilla with egg, cheese, and black beans!

This breakfast quesadilla is a satisfying and flavorful meal that's perfect for any time of day. It's filled with protein from the eggs and black beans, and the cheese adds a creamy and melty texture. Customize it with your favorite toppings and enjoy it as a hearty breakfast or brunch option!

Protein-Packed Breakfast Bread with Sunflower Seeds and Pumpkin Seeds

Ingredients:

- 1 cup all-purpose flour
- 1 cup whole wheat flour
- 1/2 cup rolled oats
- 1/4 cup sunflower seeds
- 1/4 cup pumpkin seeds
- 1/4 cup ground flaxseed
- 1/4 cup chia seeds
- 1 teaspoon baking powder
- 1/2 teaspoon baking soda
- 1/2 teaspoon salt
- 2 large eggs
- 1 cup plain Greek yogurt
- 1/4 cup honey or maple syrup
- 1/4 cup melted coconut oil or butter
- 1 teaspoon vanilla extract

Instructions:

1. Preheat your oven to 350°F (175°C). Grease a 9x5-inch loaf pan or line it with parchment paper.
2. In a large mixing bowl, combine the all-purpose flour, whole wheat flour, rolled oats, sunflower seeds, pumpkin seeds, ground flaxseed, chia seeds, baking powder, baking soda, and salt. Stir until well combined.
3. In another bowl, whisk together the eggs, Greek yogurt, honey or maple syrup, melted coconut oil or butter, and vanilla extract until smooth.
4. Pour the wet ingredients into the bowl with the dry ingredients. Stir until just combined. Be careful not to overmix.
5. Transfer the batter to the prepared loaf pan and spread it out evenly.
6. Bake in the preheated oven for 45-55 minutes, or until a toothpick inserted into the center comes out clean.
7. Remove the bread from the oven and let it cool in the pan for 10 minutes.
8. Once cooled slightly, transfer the bread to a wire rack to cool completely before slicing.

9. Slice the protein-packed breakfast bread and enjoy it plain or with your favorite toppings such as nut butter, jam, or fresh fruit.
10. Store any leftovers in an airtight container at room temperature for up to 3 days, or in the refrigerator for longer freshness.
11. Enjoy your homemade protein-packed breakfast bread with sunflower seeds and pumpkin seeds!

This protein-packed breakfast bread is loaded with seeds and whole grains, making it a nutritious and filling option for breakfast or snack time. It's easy to make and can be customized with your favorite seeds and nuts. Enjoy it toasted or plain, with your favorite toppings!

Peanut Butter Protein Pancakes with Greek Yogurt Topping

Ingredients:

For the pancakes:

- 1 cup all-purpose flour
- 1/4 cup vanilla protein powder
- 1 tablespoon sugar (optional)
- 1 teaspoon baking powder
- 1/4 teaspoon salt
- 1 cup milk (dairy or non-dairy)
- 1/4 cup creamy peanut butter
- 1 large egg
- 1 teaspoon vanilla extract

For the Greek yogurt topping:

- 1/2 cup Greek yogurt
- 1 tablespoon honey or maple syrup
- 1/2 teaspoon vanilla extract

Instructions:

1. In a large mixing bowl, whisk together the flour, protein powder, sugar (if using), baking powder, and salt.
2. In a separate microwave-safe bowl, heat the milk and peanut butter together in the microwave until the peanut butter is melted. Stir until smooth.
3. Add the melted peanut butter mixture, egg, and vanilla extract to the dry ingredients. Stir until just combined. Do not overmix; it's okay if the batter is slightly lumpy.
4. Heat a lightly greased skillet or griddle over medium heat. Pour about 1/4 cup of batter onto the skillet for each pancake.
5. Cook the pancakes for 2-3 minutes on one side, or until bubbles form on the surface and the edges begin to set.
6. Flip the pancakes and cook for an additional 1-2 minutes on the other side, until golden brown and cooked through.

7. Remove the pancakes from the skillet and repeat with the remaining batter.
8. While the pancakes are cooking, prepare the Greek yogurt topping by whisking together the Greek yogurt, honey or maple syrup, and vanilla extract in a small bowl until smooth.
9. Serve the peanut butter protein pancakes warm, topped with a dollop of Greek yogurt topping.
10. Optionally, garnish with sliced bananas, chopped nuts, or a drizzle of peanut butter.
11. Enjoy your delicious peanut butter protein pancakes with Greek yogurt topping!

These peanut butter protein pancakes are fluffy, flavorful, and packed with protein. The creamy Greek yogurt topping adds a tangy contrast and extra protein boost. They make for a satisfying and nutritious breakfast that will keep you energized throughout the morning!

High-Protein Breakfast Smoothie Bowl with Spinach and Berries

Ingredients:

For the smoothie:

- 1 ripe banana, frozen
- 1 cup mixed berries (such as strawberries, blueberries, raspberries)
- 1 cup fresh spinach leaves
- 1/2 cup plain Greek yogurt
- 1/4 cup almond milk (or any milk of your choice)
- 1 scoop vanilla protein powder
- 1 tablespoon chia seeds or ground flaxseed (optional)
- Honey or maple syrup, to taste (optional, for added sweetness)

For the toppings:

- Sliced strawberries
- Blueberries
- Raspberries
- Granola
- Sliced almonds
- Shredded coconut
- Chia seeds or hemp seeds

Instructions:

1. In a blender, combine the frozen banana, mixed berries, fresh spinach leaves, Greek yogurt, almond milk, protein powder, and chia seeds or ground flaxseed (if using). Add honey or maple syrup to taste if you prefer additional sweetness.
2. Blend the ingredients until smooth and creamy. If the mixture is too thick, you can add more almond milk, a tablespoon at a time, until you reach your desired consistency.
3. Once the smoothie is blended, pour it into a bowl.

4. Arrange your desired toppings on top of the smoothie bowl. You can use sliced strawberries, blueberries, raspberries, granola, sliced almonds, shredded coconut, and additional chia seeds or hemp seeds.
5. Serve the high-protein breakfast smoothie bowl immediately and enjoy!

This high-protein breakfast smoothie bowl with spinach and berries is not only nutritious but also delicious and satisfying. It's packed with protein from the Greek yogurt and protein powder, while the spinach adds vitamins and minerals. Feel free to customize the toppings based on your preferences and enjoy this vibrant and energizing breakfast option!

www.ingramcontent.com/pod-product-compliance
Lightning Source LLC
LaVergne TN
LVHW061945070526
838199LV00060B/3989